A Pe[illegible] That Fits

by Pauline Cartwright
illustrated by Richard Hoit

HOUGHTON MIFFLIN HARCOURT
School Publishers

Printed in China

ISBN-13: 978-0-547-25271-1
ISBN-10: 0-547-25271-4

10 11 12 0940 18 17 16 15 14 13
4500443494

Ella spent her vacation on the farm where her cousin Grace lived. Grace had a pony called Toffee. He was called Toffee because his hair was the color of toffee candy. His floppy ears twitched when he ate apples from Ella's hand.

Toffee was big. He weighed much more than Ella.

Every day, Grace and Ella brushed Toffee's coat together. They took extra care of his long, straight tail. They fed him special food, like oats and beets. He drooled when he smelled the food.

When Ella came home, she missed Toffee very much.

"Can I have a pony?" Ella asked her parents.

"We can't keep a pony in our apartment," Dad said. "A pony needs lots of space."

"A pony has to run every day, and it needs fresh air and sunshine," said Mom.

Ella was sad that she couldn't have a pony.

At breakfast Ella said, “If we moved to the country, I could have a pony!”

“How would I get to work on time?” Mom asked.

“How about finding a pet that will fit in our apartment?” Dad asked.

Ella knew her parents were right.

She was excited about choosing a pet.

The next Saturday morning, Ella asked, "Can we go to the pet store today?"

"Of course we can," said Mom and Dad.

That afternoon, they took the bus to the biggest pet store in town.

"What cute puppies!" said Ella. If we got a puppy, we could buy dog toys and collars, too.

"Our apartment is too small for a dog," said Mom.

There were a hundred different kinds of pets. Ella stood and looked at kittens, frogs, turtles, birds, goldfish, rabbits, and even mice with curly tails!

There were so many animals in a row that Ella didn't know which pet to choose. She needed a small pet, but which animal would be best? It was hard to decide.

The birds were all chirping and squawking. Then Ella heard a song. Which bird was singing?

Ella found a bright yellow canary. He started to sing his song again, and Ella thought he was singing just for her. It was the most beautiful sound she had ever heard. Finally, Ella knew which pet she wanted.

Ella carried the canary home in a new cage. The other children on the bus smiled at Ella's bird. Ella was very happy with her new pet.

"I'm going to call him Sunny because he's yellow like the sun," said Ella.

At home, Dad hung Sunny's cage up in the living room. Sunny sang loudly.

"Listen to him sing!" said Mom.

"I think Sunny will fit in just fine!" said Ella.

Responding

TARGET SKILL Sequence of Events

Ella wanted a pet. Think about what happened first, next, and last in the story. Copy the chart below. Use the chart to write three events from the story in order.

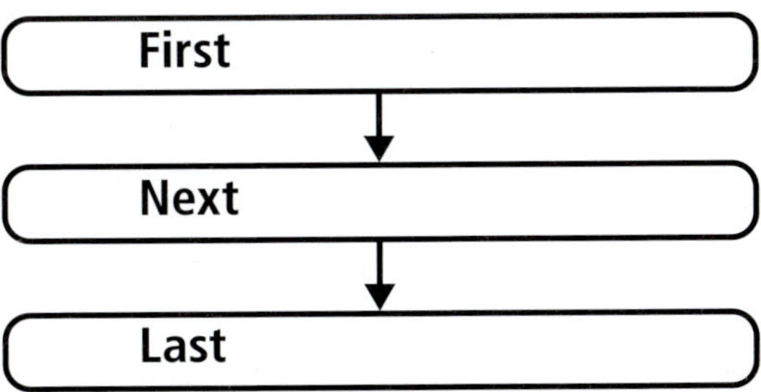

Write About It

Text to Self Think about what kind of animal you would pick to be your pet. Write a story that tells the steps you would take to pick a pet. Use time order words to add details to your story.

TARGET VOCABULARY

collars
curly
drooled
floppy
row
stood
straight
weighed

EXPAND YOUR VOCABULARY

apartment
canary
chirping
squawking
toffee

TARGET SKILL **Sequence of Events** Tell the order in which things happen.

TARGET STRATEGY **Infer/Predict** Use clues to figure out more about story parts.

GENRE **Realistic fiction** is a story that could happen in real life.